JAMES CHRISTMAS COLORING BOOK

Chiquita publishing

James's Christmas List

To: Santa
From:
JAMES

JAMES

JAMES

JAMES

JAMES

JAMES

JAMES

JAMES

JAMES

JAMES

JAMES

JAMES

JAMES

Merry Christmas
JAMES

Made in the USA
Las Vegas, NV
03 December 2021

35982914R00020